THE VISUAL CHRISTMAS STORY

To my wife, Jane,
whose life and ministry is an inspiration
and a blessing to all who know her

The Bible Reading Fellowship

15 The Chambers, Vineyard
Abingdon OX14 3FE
brf.org.uk

The Bible Reading Fellowship (BRF) is a Registered Charity (233280)

ISBN 978 0 85746 743 0
First published 2018
10 9 8 7 6 5 4 3 2 1 0
All rights reserved

Text and illustrations © Ian Long 2018
This edition © The Bible Reading Fellowship 2018

The author asserts the moral right to be identified as the author of this work

Acknowledgements

Unless otherwise stated, scripture quotations are taken from The Holy Bible, New International Version (Anglicised edition) copyright © 1979, 1984, 2011 by Biblica. Used by permission of Hodder & Stoughton Publishers, an Hachette UK company. All rights reserved. 'NIV' is a registered trademark of Biblica. UK trademark number 1448790

Every effort has been made to trace and contact copyright owners for material used in this resource. We apologise for any inadvertent omissions or errors, and would ask those concerned to contact us so that full acknowledgement can be made in the future

A catalogue record for this book is available from the British Library

Printed and bound in the UK by Zenith Media NP4 0DQ.

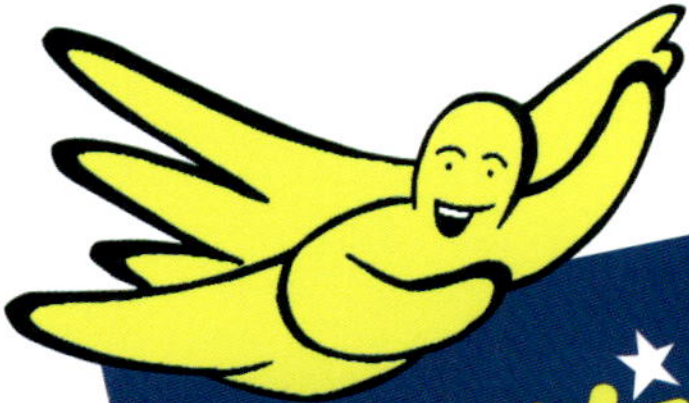

THE VISUAL CHRISTMAS STORY

Ian Long

BRF

How to use this book

Every year during Advent, Christians reflect upon the most important birthday of all time. The whole world's calendar is dated by this event. History revolves around 'His story'. The words of the Bible are familiar to many, through seasonal carols and well-attended services.

This small book attempts to bring something fresh to the Christmas account. We remember only 10% of what we hear, while we recall 40% of what we see. This is a 'visual translation' to accompany the words of the Bible and to open it up to a wider audience. Most people are visual learners, especially in our age of mass communication.

For many of the two and a half billion Christians around the world, especially those who cannot read or are still young, this book may be used as an aid to their understanding of the Christmas events. Every verse in the Bible relating to the birth of Jesus has been translated with images. Families can use it as an aid to their reflections in the morning or as a book to finish the day. Those who wish to share the origins of

Christmas with their colleagues can do so in a new way. For those who struggle to read, they can follow their own version of the Bible for the first time. For gatherings where there is more than one language, this visual translation can be a common starting point.

Most of all, as the author, I hope and pray that you will allow the images, which are an attempt to portray the meaning of the scripture as accurately as possible, to reveal something original about the God who began the greatest adventure of all by choosing to become one of us – a precious baby boy.

Ian Long

May the kings of Tarshish and of distant shores
   bring tribute to him.
May the kings of Sheba and Seba
   present him gifts.
May all kings bow down to him
   and all nations serve him.

Psalm 72:10–11

'Therefore the Lord himself will give you a sign: The virgin will conceive and give birth to a son, and will call him Immanuel.'

Isaiah 7:14

The people walking in darkness
 have seen a great light;
on those living in the land of deep darkness
 a light has dawned.

Isaiah 9:2

For to us a child is born,
   to us a son is given,
   and the government will be on his shoulders.
And he will be called
   Wonderful Counsellor, Mighty God,
   Everlasting Father, Prince of Peace.

Isaiah 9:6

A voice of one calling:
'In the wilderness prepare
　the way for the Lord;
make straight in the desert
　a highway for our God.
Every valley shall be raised up,
　every mountain and hill made low;
the rough ground shall become level,
　the rugged places a plain.'

Isaiah 40:3–4

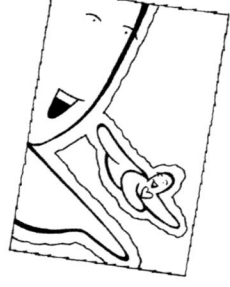

This is what the Lord says:

'A voice is heard in Ramah,
  mourning and great weeping,
Rachel weeping for her children
  and refusing to be comforted,
  because they are no more.'

Jeremiah 31:15

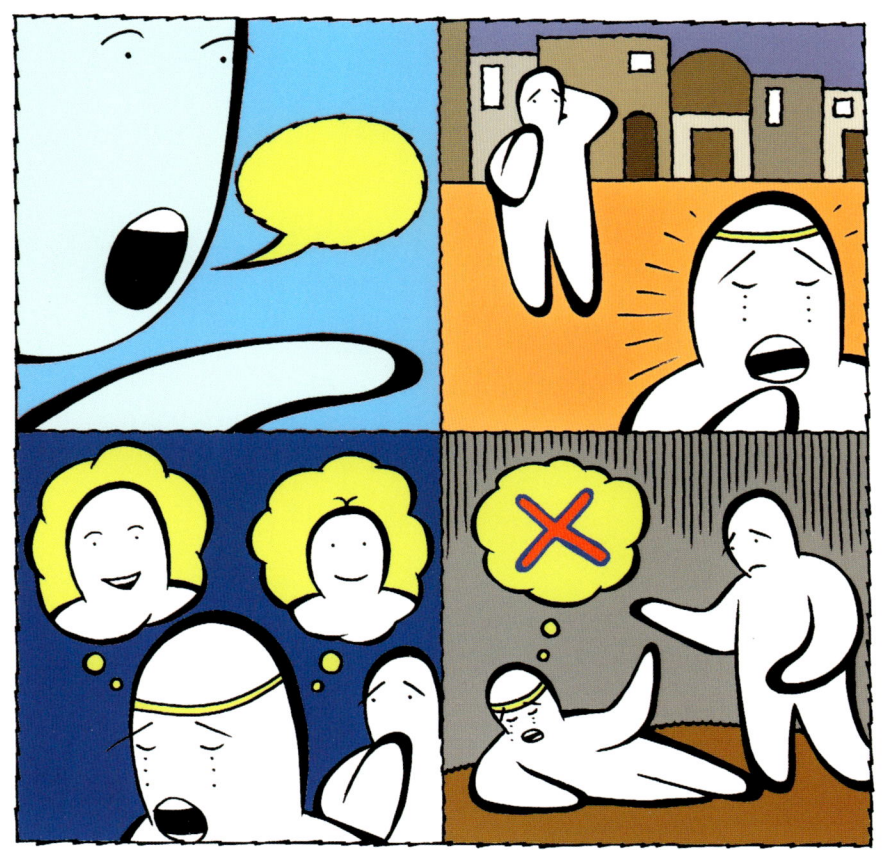

'But you, Bethlehem Ephrathah,
   though you are small among the clans of Judah,
out of you will come for me
   one who will be ruler over Israel,
whose origins are from of old,
   from ancient times.'

Therefore Israel will be abandoned
   until the time when she who is in labour bears a son,
and the rest of his brothers return
   to join the Israelites.

Micah 5:2–3

THE STORY according to Matthew

This is how the birth of Jesus the Messiah came about: his mother Mary was pledged to be married to Joseph, but before they came together, she was found to be pregnant through the Holy Spirit. Because Joseph her husband was faithful to the law, and yet did not want to expose her to public disgrace, he had in mind to divorce her quietly.

But after he had considered this, an angel of the Lord appeared to him in a dream and said, 'Joseph son of David, do not be afraid to take Mary home as your wife, because what is conceived in her is from the Holy Spirit. She will give birth to a son, and you are to give him the name Jesus, because he will save his people from their sins.'

All this took place to fulfil what the Lord had said through the prophet: 'The virgin will conceive and give birth to a son, and they will call him Immanuel' (which means 'God with us').

Matthew 1:18–23

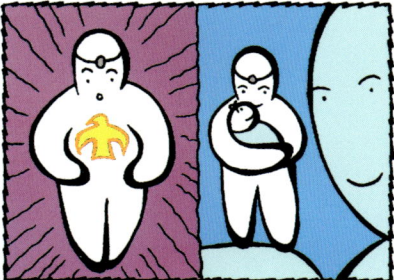

When Joseph woke up, he did what the angel of the Lord had commanded him and took Mary home as his wife. But he did not consummate their marriage until she gave birth to a son. And he gave him the name Jesus.

Matthew 1:24–25

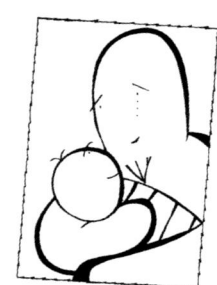

After Jesus was born in Bethlehem in Judea, during the time of King Herod, Magi from the east came to Jerusalem and asked, 'Where is the one who has been born king of the Jews? We saw his star when it rose and have come to worship him.'

Matthew 2:1–2

When King Herod heard this he was disturbed, and all Jerusalem with him. When he had called together all the people's chief priests and teachers of the law, he asked them where the Messiah was to be born. 'In Bethlehem in Judea,' they replied, 'for this is what the prophet has written:

'"But you, Bethlehem, in the land of Judah,
   are by no means least among the rulers of Judah;
for out of you will come a ruler
   who will shepherd my people Israel."'

Then Herod called the Magi secretly and found out from them the exact time the star had appeared. He sent them to Bethlehem and said, 'Go and search carefully for the child. As soon as you find him, report to me, so that I too may go and worship him.'

Matthew 2:3–8

After they had heard the king, they went on their way, and the star they had seen when it rose went ahead of them until it stopped over the place where the child was. When they saw the star, they were overjoyed.

Matthew 2:9–10

On coming to the house, they saw the child with his mother Mary, and they bowed down and worshipped him. Then they opened their treasures and presented him with gifts of gold, frankincense and myrrh. And having been warned in a dream not to go back to Herod, they returned to their country by another route.

When they had gone, an angel of the Lord appeared to Joseph in a dream. 'Get up,' he said, 'take the child and his mother and escape to Egypt. Stay there until I tell you, for Herod is going to search for the child to kill him.'

So he got up, took the child and his mother during the night and left for Egypt, where he stayed until the death of Herod. And so was fulfilled what the Lord had said through the prophet: 'Out of Egypt I called my son.'

Matthew 2:11–15

When Herod realised that he had been outwitted by the Magi, he was furious, and he gave orders to kill all the boys in Bethlehem and its vicinity who were two years old and under, in accordance with the time he had learned from the Magi. Then what was said through the prophet Jeremiah was fulfilled:

'A voice is heard in Ramah,
  weeping and great mourning,
Rachel weeping for her children
  and refusing to be comforted,
  because they are no more.'

Matthew 2:16–18

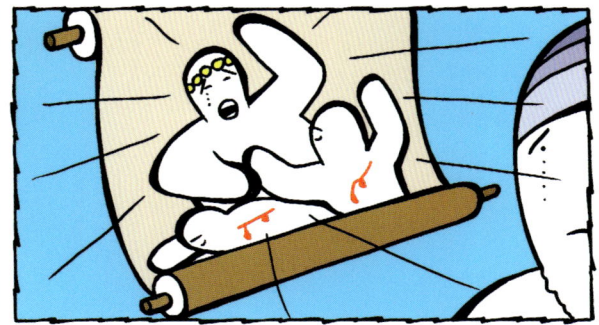

After Herod died, an angel of the Lord appeared in a dream to Joseph in Egypt and said, 'Get up, take the child and his mother and go to the land of Israel, for those who were trying to take the child's life are dead.'

So he got up, took the child and his mother and went to the land of Israel. But when he heard that Archelaus was reigning in Judea in place of his father Herod, he was afraid to go there. Having been warned in a dream, he withdrew to the district of Galilee, and he went and lived in a town called Nazareth. So was fulfilled what was said through the prophets, that he would be called a Nazarene.

Matthew 2:19–23

THE STORY according to Luke

Many have undertaken to draw up an account of the things that have been fulfilled among us, just as they were handed down to us by those who from the first were eyewitnesses and servants of the word. With this in mind, since I myself have carefully investigated everything from the beginning, I too decided to write an orderly account for you, most excellent Theophilus, so that you may know the certainty of the things you have been taught.

In the time of Herod king of Judea there was a priest named Zechariah, who belonged to the priestly division of Abijah; his wife Elizabeth was also a descendant of Aaron. Both of them were righteous in the sight of God, observing all the Lord's commands and decrees blamelessly. But they were childless because Elizabeth was not able to conceive, and they were both very old.

Once when Zechariah's division was on duty and he was serving as priest before God, he was chosen by lot, according to the custom of the priesthood, to go into the temple of the Lord and burn incense. And when the time for the burning of incense came, all the assembled worshippers were praying outside.

Luke 1:1–10

Then an angel of the Lord appeared to him, standing at the right side of the altar of incense. When Zechariah saw him, he was startled and was gripped with fear. But the angel said to him: 'Do not be afraid, Zechariah; your prayer has been heard. Your wife Elizabeth will bear you a son, and you are to call him John.'

Luke 1:11–13

'He will be a joy and delight to you, and many will rejoice because of his birth, for he will be great in the sight of the Lord. He is never to take wine or other fermented drink, and he will be filled with the Holy Spirit even before he is born. He will bring back many of the people of Israel to the Lord their God.'

Luke 1:14–16

'And he will go on before the Lord, in the spirit and power of Elijah, to turn the hearts of the parents to their children and the disobedient to the wisdom of the righteous – to make ready a people prepared for the Lord.'

Zechariah asked the angel, 'How can I be sure of this? I am an old man and my wife is well along in years.'

The angel said to him, 'I am Gabriel. I stand in the presence of God, and I have been sent to speak to you and to tell you this good news. And now you will be silent and not able to speak until the day this happens, because you did not believe my words, which will come true at their appointed time.'

Meanwhile, the people were waiting for Zechariah and wondering why he stayed so long in the temple. When he came out, he could not speak to them. They realised he had seen a vision in the temple, for he kept making signs to them but remained unable to speak.

When his time of service was completed, he returned home. After this his wife Elizabeth became pregnant and for five months remained in seclusion. 'The Lord has done this for me,' she said. 'In these days he has shown his favour and taken away my disgrace among the people.'

Luke 1:17–25

In the sixth month of Elizabeth's pregnancy, God sent the angel Gabriel to Nazareth, a town in Galilee, to a virgin pledged to be married to a man named Joseph, a descendant of David. The virgin's name was Mary.

Luke 1:26–27

The angel went to her and said, 'Greetings, you who are highly favoured! The Lord is with you.'

Mary was greatly troubled at his words and wondered what kind of greeting this might be. But the angel said to her, 'Do not be afraid, Mary; you have found favour with God. You will conceive and give birth to a son, and you are to call him Jesus. He will be great and will be called the Son of the Most High. The Lord God will give him the throne of his father David, and he will reign over Jacob's descendants forever; his kingdom will never end.'

Luke 1:28–33

'How will this be,' Mary asked the angel, 'since I am a virgin?'

The angel answered, 'The Holy Spirit will come on you, and the power of the Most High will overshadow you. So the holy one to be born will be called the Son of God. Even Elizabeth your relative is going to have a child in her old age, and she who was said to be unable to conceive is in her sixth month. For no word from God will ever fail.'

'I am the Lord's servant,' Mary answered. 'May your word to me be fulfilled.' Then the angel left her.

Luke 1:34–38

At that time Mary got ready and hurried to a town in the hill country of Judea, where she entered Zechariah's home and greeted Elizabeth.

Luke 1:39–40

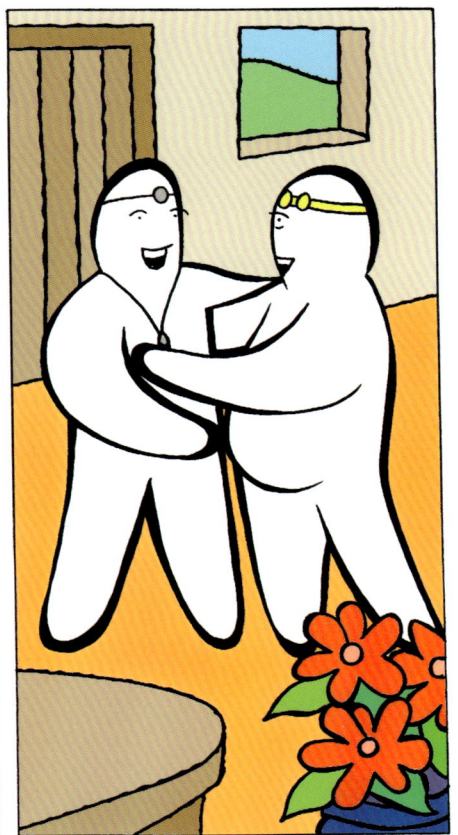

When Elizabeth heard Mary's greeting, the baby leaped in her womb, and Elizabeth was filled with the Holy Spirit. In a loud voice she exclaimed: 'Blessed are you among women, and blessed is the child you will bear! But why am I so favoured, that the mother of my Lord should come to me? As soon as the sound of your greeting reached my ears, the baby in my womb leaped for joy. Blessed is she who has believed that the Lord would fulfil his promises to her!'

Luke 1:41–45

And Mary said:

'My soul glorifies the Lord
    and my spirit rejoices in God my Saviour,
for he has been mindful
    of the humble state of his servant.
From now on all generations will call me blessed.'

Luke 1:46–48

'For the Mighty One has done great things for me –
　holy is his name.
His mercy extends to those who fear him,
　from generation to generation.
He has performed mighty deeds with his arm;
　he has scattered those who are proud in their inmost thoughts.
He has brought down rulers from their thrones
　but has lifted up the humble.
He has filled the hungry with good things
　but has sent the rich away empty.
He has helped his servant Israel,
　remembering to be merciful
to Abraham and his descendants forever,
　just as he promised our ancestors.'

Luke 1:49–55

Mary stayed with Elizabeth for about three months and then returned home.

When it was time for Elizabeth to have her baby, she gave birth to a son. Her neighbours and relatives heard that the Lord had shown her great mercy, and they shared her joy.

On the eighth day they came to circumcise the child, and they were going to name him after his father Zechariah, but his mother spoke up and said, 'No! He is to be called John.'

They said to her, 'There is no one among your relatives who has that name.'

Then they made signs to his father, to find out what he would like to name the child. He asked for a writing tablet, and to everyone's astonishment he wrote, 'His name is John.'

Luke 1:56–63

Immediately his mouth was opened and his tongue set free, and he began to speak, praising God. All the neighbours were filled with awe, and throughout the hill country of Judea people were talking about all these things. Everyone who heard this wondered about it, asking, 'What then is this child going to be?' For the Lord's hand was with him.

His father Zechariah was filled with the Holy Spirit and prophesied:

'Praise be to the Lord, the God of Israel,
  because he has come to his people and redeemed them.
He has raised up a horn of salvation for us
  in the house of his servant David
(as he said through his holy prophets of long ago),
salvation from our enemies
  and from the hand of all who hate us.'

Luke 1:64–71

'… to show mercy to our ancestors
   and to remember his holy covenant,
   the oath he swore to our father Abraham:
to rescue us from the hand of our enemies,
   and to enable us to serve him without fear
   in holiness and righteousness before him all our days.

And you, my child, will be called a prophet of the Most High;
   for you will go on before the Lord to prepare the way for him,
to give his people the knowledge of salvation
   through the forgiveness of their sins,
because of the tender mercy of our God,
   by which the rising sun will come to us from heaven
to shine on those living in darkness
   and in the shadow of death,
to guide our feet into the path of peace.'

And the child grew and became strong in spirit; and he lived in the wilderness until he appeared publicly to Israel.

Luke 1:72–80

In those days Caesar Augustus issued a decree that a census should be taken of the entire Roman world. (This was the first census that took place while Quirinius was governor of Syria.) And everyone went to their own town to register.

So Joseph also went up from the town of Nazareth in Galilee to Judea, to Bethlehem the town of David, because he belonged to the house and line of David. He went there to register with Mary, who was pledged to be married to him and was expecting a child.

Luke 2:1–5

While they were there, the time came for the baby to be born, and she gave birth to her firstborn, a son. She wrapped him in cloths and placed him in a manger, because there was no guest room available for them.

Luke 2:6–7

And there were shepherds living out in the fields nearby, keeping watch over their flocks at night. An angel of the Lord appeared to them, and the glory of the Lord shone around them, and they were terrified.

Luke 2:8–9

But the angel said to them, 'Do not be afraid. I bring you good news that will cause great joy for all the people.'

Luke 2:10

'Today in the town of David a Saviour has been born to you; he is the Messiah, the Lord. This will be a sign to you: you will find a baby wrapped in cloths and lying in a manger.'

Suddenly a great company of the heavenly host appeared with the angel, praising God and saying,

'Glory to God in the highest heaven,
   and on earth peace to those on whom his favour rests.'

When the angels had left them and gone into heaven, the shepherds said to one another, 'Let's go to Bethlehem and see this thing that has happened, which the Lord has told us about.'

So they hurried off and found Mary and Joseph, and the baby, who was lying in the manger. When they had seen him, they spread the word concerning what had been told them about this child, and all who heard it were amazed at what the shepherds said to them. But Mary treasured up all these things and pondered them in her heart. The shepherds returned, glorifying and praising God for all the things they had heard and seen, which were just as they had been told.

Luke 2:11–20

On the eighth day, when it was time to circumcise the child, he was named Jesus, the name the angel had given him before he was conceived.

When the time came for the purification rites required by the Law of Moses, Joseph and Mary took him to Jerusalem to present him to the Lord (as it is written in the Law of the Lord, 'Every firstborn male is to be consecrated to the Lord'), and to offer a sacrifice in keeping with what is said in the Law of the Lord: 'a pair of doves or two young pigeons.'

Luke 2:21–24

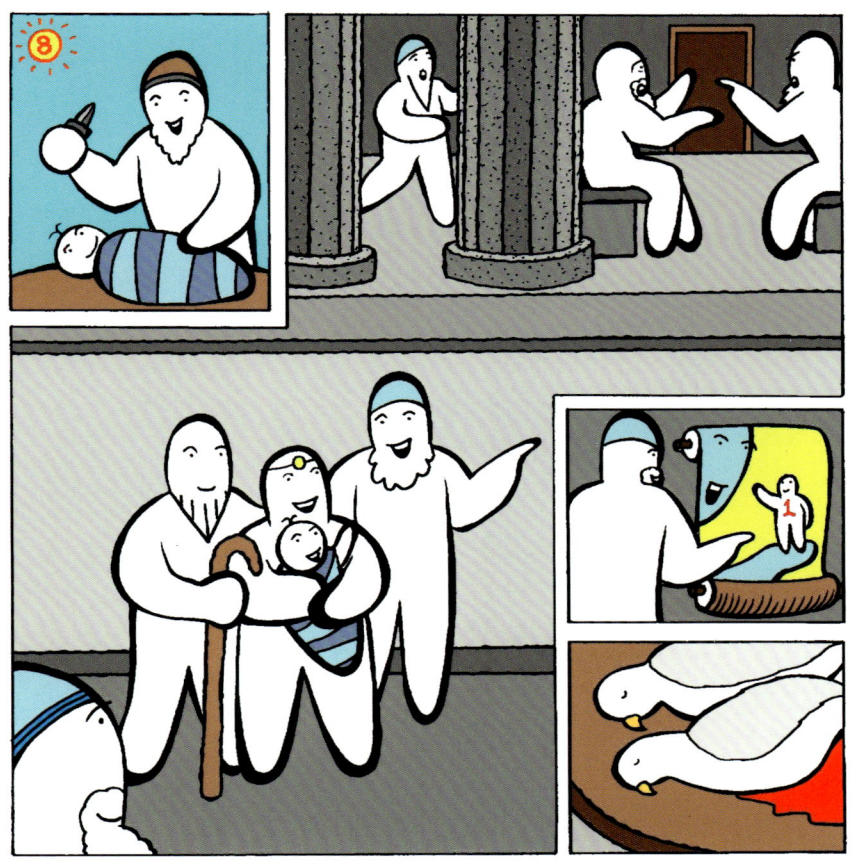

Now there was a man in Jerusalem called Simeon, who was righteous and devout. He was waiting for the consolation of Israel, and the Holy Spirit was on him. It had been revealed to him by the Holy Spirit that he would not die before he had seen the Lord's Messiah. Moved by the Spirit, he went into the temple courts. When the parents brought in the child Jesus to do for him what the custom of the Law required…

Luke 2:25–27

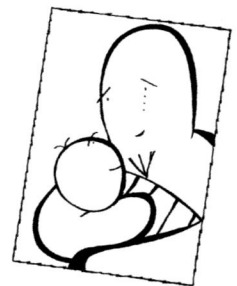

… Simeon took him in his arms and praised God, saying:

'Sovereign Lord, as you have promised,
 you may now dismiss your servant in peace.
For my eyes have seen your salvation,
 which you have prepared in the sight of all nations:
a light for revelation to the Gentiles,
 and the glory of your people Israel.'

The child's father and mother marvelled at what was said about him. Then Simeon blessed them and said to Mary, his mother: 'This child is destined to cause the falling and rising of many in Israel, and to be a sign that will be spoken against, so that the thoughts of many hearts will be revealed. And a sword will pierce your own soul too.'

There was also a prophet, Anna, the daughter of Penuel, of the tribe of Asher. She was very old; she had lived with her husband seven years after her marriage…

Luke 2:28–36

… and then was a widow until she was eighty-four. She never left the temple but worshipped night and day, fasting and praying. Coming up to them at that very moment, she gave thanks to God and spoke about the child to all who were looking forward to the redemption of Jerusalem.

When Joseph and Mary had done everything required by the Law of the Lord, they returned to Galilee to their own town of Nazareth. And the child grew and became strong; he was filled with wisdom, and the grace of God was on him.

Luke 2:37–40

Every year Jesus' parents went to Jerusalem for the Festival of the Passover. When he was twelve years old, they went up to the festival, according to the custom. After the festival was over, while his parents were returning home, the boy Jesus stayed behind in Jerusalem, but they were unaware of it. Thinking he was in their company, they travelled on for a day. Then they began looking for him among their relatives and friends.

Luke 2:41–44

When they did not find him, they went back to Jerusalem to look for him. After three days they found him in the temple courts, sitting among the teachers, listening to them and asking them questions. Everyone who heard him was amazed at his understanding and his answers. When his parents saw him, they were astonished. His mother said to him, 'Son, why have you treated us like this? Your father and I have been anxiously searching for you.'

'Why were you searching for me?' he asked. 'Didn't you know I had to be in my Father's house?' But they did not understand what he was saying to them.

Then he went down to Nazareth with them and was obedient to them. But his mother treasured all these things in her heart. And Jesus grew in wisdom and stature, and in favour with God and man.

Luke 2:45–52

THE STORY according to JOHN

In the beginning was the Word, and the Word was with God, and the Word was God. He was with God in the beginning. Through him all things were made; without him nothing was made that has been made. In him was life, and that life was the light of all mankind. The light shines in the darkness, and the darkness has not overcome it.

John 1:1–5

There was a man sent from God whose name was John. He came as a witness to testify concerning that light, so that through him all might believe. He himself was not the light; he came only as a witness to the light.

The true light that gives light to everyone was coming into the world. He was in the world, and though the world was made through him, the world did not recognise him. He came to that which was his own, but his own did not receive him. Yet to all who did receive him, to those who believed in his name, he gave the right to become children of God – children born not of natural descent, nor of human decision or a husband's will, but born of God.

John 1:6–13

The Word became flesh and made his dwelling among us. We have seen his glory, the glory of the one and only Son, who came from the Father, full of grace and truth.

John 1:14

For God so loved the world that he gave his one and only Son, that whoever believes in him shall not perish but have eternal life.

John 3:16

An affirming Christmas gift for families to use at home over the Christmas holiday period. This minibook aims to transfer the core values of Messy Church to the home and family context, encouraging families to talk together, be creative, be hospitable, be Christ-centred and celebratory, and including activities for all ages.

Christmas Family Time
Lucy Moore with Jane Leadbetter and Martyn Payne
978 0 85746 521 4 £1.99
brfonline.org.uk

Love God… Love your neighbour… Love yourself. The gospel is good news for messy people, young and old, and this resource is designed for those who are ready to make it their own. Written in an interactive, user-friendly and jargon-free style, it helps individuals and families alike to take the next steps in their Christian journey.

Family Jesus Time
Going on the faith adventure
Lucy Moore with Jane Leadbetter and Martyn Payne
978 0 85746 675 4 £1.99
brfonline.org.uk

BRF

Transforming
lives and communities

Christian growth and understanding of the Bible

Resourcing individuals, groups and leaders in churches for their own spiritual journey and for their ministry

Church outreach in the local community

Offering two programmes that churches are embracing to great effect as they seek to engage with their local communities and transform lives

Teaching Christianity in primary schools

Working with children and teachers to explore Christianity creatively and confidently

Children's and family ministry

Working with churches and families to explore Christianity creatively and bring the Bible alive

Visit **brf.org.uk** for more information on BRF's work

brf.org.uk

The Bible Reading Fellowship (BRF) is a Registered Charity (No. 233280)